Science in the Schoolyard

Preschool–Kindergarten

Table of Contents

About This Book

What better way to foster youngsters' natural curiosity about the world around them than with fun science activities to do both outdoors and in the classroom? *Science in the Schoolyard* is a collection of 31 easy-to-implement seasonal science activities, experiments, observations, and demonstrations. These thought-provoking activities are developmentally appropriate and cover a variety of earth, life, and physical science topics. Each two-page unit includes a colorful step-by-step instruction sheet for the teacher and a reproducible recording sheet or pattern for students. These seasonal activities require little preparation time and the pick-and-choose nature of this book will help you select the perfect activities to complement your existing science curriculum.

Managing Editor: Cindy Daoust
Editor at Large: Diane Badden
Staff Editor: Michele Dare de Miranda
Contributing Writers: Melissa Hauck Bryan, Jill Davis, Kristin Bauer Ganoung, Ada Goren, Lucia Kemp Henry, Alison LaManna, Suzanne Moore
Copy Editors: Tazmen Carlisle, Gina Farago, Karen Brewer Grossman, Amy Kirtley-Hill, Karen L. Mayworth, Kristy Parton, Debbie Shoffner, Cathy Edwards Simrell
Cover Artist: Clevell Harris, Ivy L. Koonce, Barry Slate
Art Coordinator: Clint Moore
Artists: Pam Crane, Theresa Lewis Goode, Nick Greenwood, Clevell Harris, Ivy L. Koonce, Sheila Krill, Clint Moore, Greg D. Rieves, Rebecca Saunders, Barry Slate, Donna K. Teal
The Mailbox® Books.com: Jennifer Tipton Bennett (DESIGNER/ARTIST); Stuart Smith (PRODUCTION ARTIST); Karen White (EDITORIAL ASSISTANT); Paul Fleetwood, Xiaoyun Wu (SYSTEMS)

President, The Mailbox Book Company™: Joseph C. Bucci
Director of Book Planning and Development: Chris Poindexter
Curriculum Director: Karen P. Shelton
Book Development Managers: Cayce Guiliano, Elizabeth H. Lindsay, Thad McLaurin
Editorial Planning: Kimberley Bruck (MANAGER); Debra Liverman, Sharon Murphy, Susan Walker (TEAM LEADERS)
Editorial and Freelance Management: Karen A. Brudnak, Hope Rodgers (EDITORIAL ASSISTANT)
Editorial Production: Lisa K. Pitts (TRAFFIC MANAGER); Lynette Dickerson (TYPE SYSTEMS); Mark Rainey (TYPESETTER)
Librarian: Dorothy C. McKinney

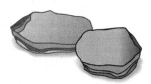

www.themailbox.com

©2003 by THE EDUCATION CENTER, INC.
All rights reserved.
ISBN# 1-56234-549-4

Manufactured in the United States
10 9 8 7 6 5 4 3 2 1

Lovely Leaves

Mix math and science with this exploration of autumn leaves.

Purpose: To help students understand why leaves change color

Background: Leaves of deciduous trees are green because they contain a pigment called chlorophyll, which helps them make food. In autumn, the chlorophyll breaks down. Then other pigments—which have always been there but have been masked by the green of the chlorophyll—can be seen. The color of an autumn leaf depends upon which pigment is most plentiful in the leaf.

Getting started: On a bright autumn day, take your youngsters outdoors for a walk. Give each child a large zippered plastic bag or a small paper sack in which to collect leaves. As students collect leaves, talk about why the leaves aren't all green. Explain why leaves change color at this time of year. Then return to your classroom with the leaves to complete the lesson.

Materials for each child:
copy of page 4
leaves collected on walk
crayons

Steps:
1. Read aloud the color words on page 4 and have each child color the leaves accordingly.
2. Ask each child to sort the leaves he has collected into color groups corresponding to those on the page.
3. Have him make tally marks to show the number of leaves he has in each color group.
4. Have each child count the tally marks for each color. Discuss the results. Who has more red leaves? Who has more yellow ones?

This is why: Autumn brings cooler temperatures and changes in sunlight. This change in season is why chlorophyll breaks down, allowing leaves' hidden colors to show.

Suggested book: *Why Do Leaves Change Colors?* by Betsy Maestro

Lovely Leaves

Color. Sort. Tally.

red

yellow

orange

brown

green

other

Fall: leaves

Wind Watchers

Watching the wind is wild indeed—sometimes it's barely there and sometimes it has great speed!

Purpose: To help students understand that the effects of wind can be observed

Background: Wind is moving air. The rising of warm air and then cold air rushing in creates wind. When air moves slowly, the gentle wind is called a breeze. When air moves fast, the strong wind is called a gale.

Getting started: Help each child make a streamer by taping crepe paper onto a straw. Discuss with youngsters how they can tell when the wind is blowing. Invite them outdoors on a windy day to observe the wind blowing trees, plants, flags, and themselves! Guide youngsters to conclude that they can see the effects of wind even though they can't see wind itself. To complete this experiment, help youngsters follow the steps below to test the wind for five consecutive days.

Materials for each child:
copy of page 6
12" length of crepe paper
a straw
access to tape
six 2" lengths of yarn

Steps:
1. Have each child choose a spot to stand outside and hold her streamer out in front of her body. Does the streamer move? Is it moving to the left or to the right?
2. Help each child record her observation by gluing a piece of yarn in the space provided on her sheet to show the effect of wind that day. Then help her write or dictate the day on the line provided on the sheet.
3. Repeat Steps 1 and 2 on each consecutive day that week, making sure each child stands facing the same direction each day.
4. On the fifth day, help each child review her sheet. Did the wind blow the same direction each day? Was it gentle or strong? Ask her to predict what the wind direction may be tomorrow and then glue a piece of yarn in the last square to show her answer.

This is why: The wind may blow so gently that you can hardly feel it, or it might blow hard enough to push over a tree. Winds are named according to the direction they are blowing from: north, south, east, or west. Wind is also a part of weather. Wind direction can often give an idea of what weather is coming because the wind often carries weather from place to place. North winds usually bring cold air. South winds generally bring warm air. East winds may bring cloudy skies. West winds often bring fair weather.

Suggested book: *Can You See the Wind?* by Allan Fowler

Name _____

Wind Watchers

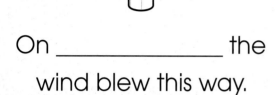 Write. ☐ Glue.

On _____ the
wind blew this way.

On _____ the
wind blew this way.

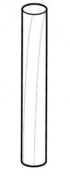
On _____ the
wind blew this way.

On _____ the
wind blew this way.
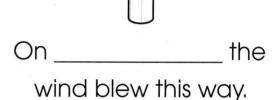

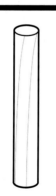
On _____ the
wind blew this way.

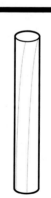
Tomorrow the wind may
blow this way.

The Great Pumpkin!

How do pumpkins grow? After observing changes in planted seeds, your little punkins will know!

Purpose: To help students understand that pumpkins grow from the seeds that are produced inside the pumpkins.

Background: Pumpkins are members of the squash family. The pumpkin plant produces round or oval fruits called pumpkins. Every pumpkin produces many seeds that can be planted to grow new pumpkins. Pumpkins are harvested during the fall and are used in a variety of ways, such as in cooking and baking and for carving. Their seeds can be used for snacks.

Getting started: In advance, obtain a small pumpkin and cut a circle around the stem to make a lid. Then take it and all the materials outside. Invite youngsters to sit around the pumpkin and observe its color, shape, and size; then count the number of lines running from top to bottom. Ask youngsters to describe what they think is inside the pumpkin. Remove the pumpkin top and ask youngsters to use their senses to describe their observations. Encourage each student to take a handful of seeds out of the pumpkin, place them on his plate, and count them. Students will be amazed at the number of seeds within one pumpkin! Then set out a tub of water and help students follow the steps below to complete the activity.

Materials for each child:
2 copies of page 8
8 oz. clear plastic cup with a pencil hole poked in the bottom
pumpkin seed
potting soil to fill the cup
plastic wrap to cover the cup
rubber band
small foam plate
crayons
access to a water spray bottle
permanent marker to share

Steps:
1. Have each child write his name on a cup and then fill it with soil.
2. Help him remove the pulp from a seed and then rinse it in water.
3. Demonstrate how to push the seed into the soil along the side of the cup so the seed is visible.
4. Have him use the spray bottle to saturate the soil with water.
5. Help each child cover his cup with plastic wrap and then secure it with a rubber band.
6. Have him write "1" in the first square on his recording sheet and then draw a picture of his seed in the first cup. Then help him write or dictate to describe his illustration.
7. Have each child put his cup on a foam plate and place it near a sunny window.
8. Encourage each child to observe his plant over the next few days and record growth on his sheet. When seed leaves poke through the top of the soil (about seven days), remove the plastic wrap and have each child continue to water his plant and record growth on his sheet.

This is why: Every pumpkin seed contains a tiny plant curled up inside it. When the seed is planted in warm, moist soil, the root grows down into the soil, where it takes in water and food for the plant. Then two seed leaves push up through the soil to soak up the sunlight. The new tiny plant is called a seedling.

Suggested book: *Life Cycle of a Pumpkin* by Ron Fridell and Patricia Walsh

Name _____

 # My Pumpkin Seed Growth

Day

[ ]

What I See

_____
_____
_____
_____

Day

[ ]

What I See

_____
_____
_____
_____

Day

[ ]

What I See

_____
_____
_____

Nutty Collection

Your little ones will chatter with excitement with this squirrely activity!

Purpose: To help youngsters understand that some squirrels work hard to gather and store food for winter

Background: Some squirrels gather and store nuts and seeds during the fall season. These squirrels stockpile their food underground or under leaves or brush. A good memory and a keen sense of smell help them retrieve hidden food, even when it is buried under snow. The nuts that they do not find often grow into new trees.

Getting started: In advance, scatter a bag of unshelled peanuts (substitute packing peanuts if any child in your class has peanut allergies) in a clear open space outdoors. After sharing some of the background information with students, take them outside and show them the border of the gathering area. Tell youngsters that they are going to gather nuts two different ways, first as themselves and then pretending to be squirrels.

Materials for each child:
copy of page 10 clipped onto a piece of cardboard
personalized paper bowl
crayon

Steps:
1. Have each child carry her bowl with her and gather nuts for one minute.
2. Have her count the nuts and then draw and write to record the number on her sheet. Have each child toss her nuts back into the open area to prepare for the second round of gathering.
3. Have each child set her bowl along the border of the gathering area. On a signal, have her pick up one nut, carry it to her bowl, and drop it in, pretending to be a squirrel taking one nut at a time back to its nesting area. Then have her return to the area to gather one more nut. Repeat this process for one minute.
4. Have each child count the nuts and record the number on her sheet.
5. Help each child compare her results. Then have her draw to answer the question at the bottom of the page.

This is why: A squirrel that scurries around to gather and store food during the fall season does so due to its sense of survival. In some areas, some types of nuts and seeds are plentiful during late fall but may be difficult to find during the winter.

Suggested book: *Nuts to You!* by Lois Ehlert

Name _____

My Nutty Collection

▭▭ Draw.

I gathered _____ nuts.

When I pretended to be a squirrel, I gathered _____ nuts.

Who works harder?

Fall: animal behavior   ©The Education Center, Inc. • *Science in the Schoolyard* • TEC917

Seasonal Senses

'Tis the season for changes! Invite youngsters to take note of fall changes with this observation activity.

Purpose: To help students understand seasonal weather changes

Background: During autumn, changes begin to occur not only in the environment but also in animals and people. The air becomes cooler. Leaves begin to change colors. Squirrels begin storing seeds and nuts. Geese and other birds head toward warmer climates. Ants move to the deepest parts of their nests. Dogs grow a thicker coat of fur. And people begin wearing jackets, sweaters, and other warm articles of clothing.

Getting started: Provide each child with a copy of the recording sheet on page 12. Discuss the seasonal changes described above and then help students follow the steps below to complete the activity.

Materials for each child:
copy of page 12
crayons

Steps:
1. Take students on a nature walk around your school grounds and instruct each child to use her senses to observe seasonal changes that have occurred.
2. Return to the classroom and invite students to review what they have seen.
3. Give each child a recording sheet and help her read the directions. Then have her draw and color as indicated on her sheet. Have each child complete her recording sheet by circling those things that she observed while on the walk.

This is why: The changes that occur during fall help nature and people prepare for the coming winter.

Suggested book: *Fall* by Ron Hirschi

Name _____

Seasonal Senses

✏️ Draw.   🖍️ Color.

Circle what you saw on the walk.

Draw ❄️❄️.

Draw 🌰🌰 in the hole.

Draw a 🐦 flying.

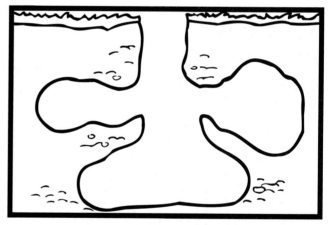

Draw 🐛 🐛.

Draw fur on the dog.

Draw a 🧥 on the child.

Full of Life

Does it grow? Does it breathe? Does it eat? Your little scientists will become experts at classifying living things and nonliving things with this observation activity.

Purpose: To help students understand the difference between living and nonliving things

Background: Living things are capable of certain activities, such as breathing, eating and drinking, growing, and reproducing.

Getting started: Discuss with youngsters what kinds of things are living and nonliving. To prepare a clipboard for each child, unfold the white sheet and then use the large clip to attach it to a piece of cardboard. Read the text on page 14 to youngsters. Then take your little scientists outside for an observation walk. Have youngsters sit in a circle and help them follow the steps below to complete the activity.

Materials for each child:
copy of page 14
sheet of white paper folded into sixths
9" x 12" piece of cardboard with a large clip
crayons
scissors
access to a stapler

Steps:
1. Give each child a clipboard and crayons.
2. Ask each child to name several objects observed and help him classify each object as living or nonliving. If desired, record students' observations on a chart.
3. Then have each child draw and color a different object on each section of his blank sheet.
4. Return to the classroom and have each child cut out his six illustrations.
5. Have each child classify and sort his illustrations as living or nonliving. Then help him staple each set onto the corresponding box on his recording sheet.
6. Encourage each child to share his completed sheet with a buddy.

This is why: When a child observes nature, he develops an understanding of what characteristics distinguish living things from nonliving things. Then the child uses that experience to recognize and classify other living and nonliving things.

Suggested book: *What's Alive?* by Kathleen Weidner

Living or Not?

Living things breathe.
Living things eat.
Living things grow.

These are living things.

These are nonliving things.

Falling Temperatures

Falling temperatures fit right in with the season!

Purpose: To help students understand that temperature changes can be observed and measured

Background: The seasons (fall, winter, spring, and summer) are caused by Earth's yearly journey around the sun along with the tilt of Earth's axis. As Earth travels around the sun, it spins on its axis, which is always tilted in the same direction. During fall, the air grows cooler in the Northern Hemisphere because it is tilted away from the sun.

Getting started: In advance, check your local weather forecast to find out when there is a cold front moving into your area and plan to do this activity then. (There should be a more dramatic change in temperature when a cold front moves in.) To prepare, set up an easy-to-read thermometer outdoors. Take your little meteorologists outside to observe seasonal changes, such as temperatures cooling, leaves changing colors and falling, squirrels gathering nuts, and caterpillars. Show youngsters the thermometer and explain that it measures the temperature of the air. Then give youngsters their recording sheets and help them follow the steps below to complete the activity.

Materials for each child:
2 copies of page 16 clipped onto a piece of cardboard
crayons

Steps:
1. Read the temperature on the thermometer as the group observes.
2. Have each child take a turn reading the temperature.
3. Help each child write the date in the space provided above one thermometer on her recording sheet. Then have her color the thermometer to record the temperature for today.
4. Repeat Steps 2 and 3 for three days.
5. Discuss with students any differences in temperature recordings over the four days.

This is why: Fall brings cooler temperatures, shorter days, and longer nights. While temperatures are not extreme during the fall season, there is a mixture of warm air and cold air. The thermometer measures the temperature of the air. When the liquid inside a thermometer gets warmer, it expands and rises up, resulting in a higher temperature reading. When the liquid inside the thermometer gets cooler, it goes down, resulting in a lower temperature reading.

Suggested book: *Whatever the Weather* by Karen Wallace

Name _____

Falling Temperatures

✏️ Write. 🖍️ Color.

┌─────────────────┐	┌─────────────────┐

50 –	–120	50 –	–120
45 –	–110	45 –	–110
40 –	–100	40 –	–100
35 –	– 90	35 –	– 90
30 –	– 80	30 –	– 80
25 –	– 70	25 –	– 70
20 –	– 60	20 –	– 60
15 –	– 50	15 –	– 50
10 –	– 40	10 –	– 40
5 –	– 30	5 –	– 30
0 –	– 20	0 –	– 20
-5 –	– 10	-5 –	– 10
-10 –	– 0	-10 –	– 0
-15 –	– -10	-15 –	– -10
-20 –	– -20	-20 –	– -20
-25 –		-25 –	
-30 –		-30 –	

C°   F°   C°   F°

The temperature is

_____ degrees.

The temperature is

_____ degrees.

Fall: temperature

Shadow Search

Shed light on shadows with this sunny observation.

Purpose: To help students understand why shadows appear

Background: The sun shines onto the earth. When an object blocks light, a shadow is cast on the ground or other surface.

Getting started: On a sunny morning, head outdoors with your students and the materials listed below. In advance, attach each copy of page 18 to a sheet of cardboard. Have students observe the shadows on the ground, including their own shadows.

Materials:
copy of page 18 for each child
black crayon for each child
lunchbox
4 different colors of sidewalk chalk

Steps:
1. Give each child a black crayon and a copy of page 18.
2. Find a spot outside that is sunny throughout the day. Use chalk to mark an X on the ground. Place the lunchbox on the X. Have students observe the shadow the lunchbox casts and then look at the position of the sun in the sky. Trace the shadow around the lunchbox with a different color of chalk. Direct each child to illustrate the shadow in the top box on her recording sheet. Then remove the lunchbox and return to the classroom.
3. An hour later, return with youngsters to the same spot. Place the lunchbox on the X and direct students to observe the shadow and the sun position. Trace the shadow with a different color of chalk. Have each child illustrate the shadow in the middle box on her recording sheet. Return to the classroom and discuss the changes in the shadow and the position of the sun.
4. An hour later, repeat Step 3, having each student illustrate the shadow in the last box.

This is why: Each day, the sun rises in the east and sets in the west. As the day progresses, the sun moves across the sky. The movement of the sun causes the size and shape of the shadows to change.

Suggested book: *What Makes a Shadow?* by Clyde Robert Bulla

Name _____

Shadow Search

 Draw the shadow.

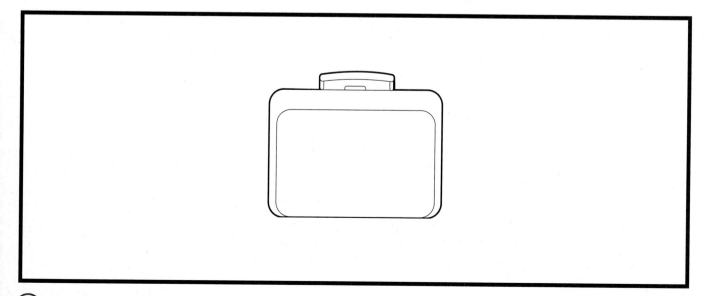

Our Five Senses

Little ones' sensible observations will help them discover the world around them.

Purpose: To help students understand the five senses

Background: Senses help us tell what is happening in the world around us. We have five main senses: sight, hearing, touch, taste, and smell.

Getting started: Mix up a batch of hot chocolate for a small group of children. Then pour it into a Thermos container. Take a small group of youngsters outside along with the Thermos container, a supply of foam cups, and the materials listed below. Find a place where youngsters can sit comfortably while they use crayons and paper. Then help them follow the steps below to complete the activity.

Materials for each child:
copy of page 20 attached to a piece of cardboard
crayons

Steps:
1. Give each child a copy of the observation chart and some crayons.
2. Ask each child to concentrate on what she can see. Have her draw in the corresponding column of her chart one outdoor thing she sees.
3. Have her dictate a sentence about her drawing; then write her response below her drawing.
4. Repeat Steps 2 and 3 for the senses of hearing and touch.
5. Encourage students to use their sense of smell to explore the environment. Then open the container of hot chocolate for students to smell.
6. Have each child follow Steps 2 and 3 to complete the fourth column on her chart.
7. Pour some hot chocolate into a cup for each child. Invite each child to taste her hot chocolate and then follow Steps 2 and 3 to complete the final column on her chart.
8. Return to the classroom and review students' charts. How many different things could students see, hear, feel, smell, and taste? Which part(s) of the body helped students use each sense? Was it difficult to concentrate on only one sense at a time?

This is why: The parts of the body that we use to sense things (the eyes, ears, skin, tongue, and nose) are called *sense organs.* Sometimes it is difficult to isolate one sense at a time. For example, the nose and tongue work closely together to help us smell and taste foods.

Suggested book: *My Five Senses* by Aliki

Name _____

My Five Senses

 Draw.

I see...	I hear...	I feel...	I smell...	I taste...

Colorful Icicles

Chilly painting during this hands-on activity introduces youngsters to the concepts of solid, liquid, and gas.

Purpose: To help students understand that water can be a solid, a liquid, or a gas

Background: Water can be a solid, a liquid, or a gas. A solid has a definite shape; a liquid has a definite volume that takes on the shape of its container; a gas has no definite shape or volume. No other substance on Earth can be found in nature in all three forms.

Getting started: Show students an example of a liquid, a solid, and a gas (such as water, ice cubes, and steam off a cup of hot chocolate). Explain to youngsters that these are all examples of water in its different forms. Then help each child follow the steps below to complete the activity.

Materials for each child:
copy of page 22
5 oz. paper cup of water
craft stick
paintbrush

square of plastic wrap to cover the cup
rubber band
tempera paints to share

Steps:
1. Have each child make colored water by dipping her paintbrush in the paint and then into her cup of water. Prepare one extra cup to use later. Tell students that water is a liquid.
2. Help each child secure the plastic wrap on her cup with the rubber band and then poke the craft stick into the middle of it.
3. Place the cups in the freezer until frozen solid, forming icicle paints.
4. Take youngsters outdoors and give them their icicle paints. Discuss with students how the liquid water changed to solid ice.
5. As youngsters observe, remove the paper cup from the extra icicle paint and place it in a sunny spot. Draw a chalk line around it.
6. Help each child peel the cup off her icicle paint. Then invite each child to paint on the sidewalk. As youngsters are painting, discuss with them how the solid icicle is melting into liquid water paint.
7. Periodically have youngsters observe the icicle placed in the sun. After the icicle has melted and the puddle has dried up, tell students that it has evaporated into a gas.
8. To review the sequence of the experiment, help each child complete a copy of page 22.

This is why: Water becomes a solid at its freezing point of 32°F. When water stands for a period of time, it gradually *evaporates,* or disappears into the air as a gas.

Suggested book: *What Is the World Made Of? All About Solids, Liquids, and Gases* by Kathleen Weidner Zoehfeld

Name _____

Water Ways

 Color.  Cut. Sequence.

Solid icicle paint

Liquid colored water

Evaporating to a gas

Melting to a liquid

Winter: solid, liquid, gas   ©The Education Center, Inc. • *Science in the Schoolyard* • TEC917

Brrr! It's Frosty!

Your little ones will chill out when they learn to make frost!

Purpose: To help students understand how frost forms

Background: Frost is a collection of ice crystals that form patterns. On nights when the air temperature falls below 32°F, water vapor settles and then freezes on windowpanes, grass, and other objects close to the ground.

Getting started: On a frosty morning, take youngsters outdoors to observe frost. Invite each child to feel frost on blades of grass. Lead youngsters in a discussion of how the frost looks and feels. Then return to the classroom to complete the lesson.

Materials:
copy of page 24 for each child
empty 16 oz. can (cover the can's rim with tape for safety)
crushed ice (enough to fill the can)
1 c. water
3 tbsp. salt
spoon
crayons or pencils
glue
clear glitter

Steps:
1. Fill the can with crushed ice and then have each child feel the outside of the can.
2. Pour the water over the ice. Have each child watch the outside of the can for several minutes.
3. When water forms on the outside of the can, have each child draw droplets on her recording sheet to resemble those on the can.
4. Add the salt to the can and use a spoon to gently stir the salt into the ice water. Wait about five minutes.
5. Have each youngster observe the thin layer of frost that forms on the outside of the can. Encourage each child to scratch the frosty layer with her fingernail.
6. Have each child illustrate the chilly results by using her finger to spread a small amount of glue on her paper. Next, invite her to sprinkle frost (glitter) over the glue and then shake off the excess.

This is why: When salt is added to the ice water the melting point of the ice is lowered, which makes the water inside the can colder. When the water gets colder, the can gets colder. The water on the outside of the can freezes, covering it with frost.

Suggested book: *When Winter Comes* by Robert Maass

Name _____

Frosty Fun

🖍 Draw.

Add GLUE .

Add ▭ .

©The Education Center, Inc. • *Science in the Schoolyard* • TEC917

Good Vibrations

Youngsters will feel good vibrations as they learn about sound with this fun demonstration.

Purpose: To help students understand sound vibration

Background: Sound begins from the *vibration* of an object. The sound makes the surrounding air, water, or other substance vibrate. The vibration travels as *sound waves* (which resemble water waves), moving outward in all directions.

Getting started: To prepare the oatmeal container, trace and cut out a circle the size of a paper towel tube from the middle of the container. Invite youngsters outside to feel their own sound vibrations. Have students place their fingers on their throats and then ask them to hum a tune, yell, and then whisper. Discuss the differences in the vibrations they feel from all three actions. Then help students follow the steps below to see the effect of sound vibrations.

Materials:
copy of page 26 for each child
round oatmeal container without the lid
class supply of paper towel tubes
12" balloon with the opening cut off
rubber band
duct tape
testing materials (pebbles, leaves, seeds, rice, beans, oatmeal, pennies)
crayons

Steps:

1. Stretch the balloon over the top of the container and secure it with a rubber band as shown. Ask a child to help tape the balloon in place.
2. Ask a child to push her paper towel tube into the hole in the oatmeal container.
3. Invite the same child to talk into her tube as another child feels the vibration on the balloon top.
4. Sprinkle one of the testing materials on top of the balloon. Then ask the child to talk or hum into her tube as other students observe. *(The testing material will move slowly or rapidly depending on the intensity of the child's voice.)* Have the child remove her tube from the container.
5. Repeat Steps 2 through 4 with each child, experimenting with each different material.
6. Discuss with youngsters why different testing materials behaved differently and how the loudness or softness of each child's voice affected the outcome. Then review the results with youngsters as you guide them to draw the experiment on their recording sheets.

This is why: The sound waves created by youngsters' voices make vibrations that cause the stretched balloon to vibrate. The testing materials are lightweight, so the vibrations cause them to bounce up and down.

Suggested book: *Sounds All Around* by Wendy Pfeffer

Good Vibrations

Draw your face. Draw your experiment.

I feel sound vibrations.

I see sound vibrations.

Pops to Puddles

How does the sun change icicles into puddles of water? Youngsters will find out with this ice pop experiment!

Purpose: To help students understand how heat causes change in temperature

Background: Temperature is a measurement of the degree of hotness or coldness of something. Heat is a form of energy that can be passed from one object to another. Heat always flows from the hotter object to the cooler object.

Getting started: On a cold winter day, take your students outside to search for icicles. Invite each child to rub his finger on an icicle. Discuss what happens when a warm finger touches the icicle. *(The icicle begins to melt and turn into water.)* Explain to students that the warmth from their bodies passes to the icicle and causes it to melt. Then help your group follow the steps below to complete the activity.

Materials:
copy of page 28 for each child   2 clear plastic cups
2 different-colored ice pops   crayons

Steps:
1. Place one ice pop upside down in a cup. Then have youngsters help find a sunny area in which to place the cup.
2. Have each child record the color of the ice pop in the appropriate section on her recording sheet.
3. Place the other ice pop upside down in the other cup. Then have youngsters help find a shady area in which to place the cup.
4. Have each child record the color of the ice pop on her sheet.
5. Return to your classroom and ask students to predict whether the ice pops will melt at the same rate.
6. Wait an hour (adjust the time according to your local temperature); then take youngsters outside to observe the changes in the ice pops.
7. Have each child record the change by coloring the liquid level on each of the cups on her sheet. Then discuss the reason for the different amounts of liquid in each cup.

This is why: The sun is a source of heat. The ice pop sitting in the sun received heat, so the temperature of the ice pop rose, causing it to melt. The ice pop in the shade did not receive as much heat, so it melted more slowly.

Suggested book: *Why Does Ice Melt?* by Jim Pipe

Name _____

Pops to Puddles

Color to show your results.

Dandy Seeds

Show youngsters one way seeds travel with an activity that's sure to blow them over!

Purpose: To help students understand how some seeds can travel by wind

Background: As a dandelion matures, the tiny individual flowers that make up the head form feathery seeds. These seeds can be carried by the wind so that the seeds can *germinate,* or grow, in new places.

Getting started: Prepare a canvas for each child by taping one square of Con-Tact paper sticky side up onto construction paper. On a calm day, take a small group of students outdoors to gather dandelions that have gone to seed. (If dandelions don't grow in your schoolyard, pick several ahead of time from an off-site location.) Have each child carefully carry one dandelion to a sidewalk or blacktop area to create some dandy dandelion art!

Materials for each child:
copy of page 32
crayons
dandelion that has gone to seed

9" x 12" sheet of construction paper
two 5" squares of clear Con-Tact paper
tape

Steps:
1. Set the canvas on the sidewalk or blacktop. Have each child hold her dandelion and stand two or three feet away from her canvas.
2. Have her blow gently on the dandelion and observe how many tiny seeds fly through the air and drift onto her canvas. Then have her illustrate her findings in the first box on her recording sheet.
3. Have her stand near her canvas again and blow hard on her dandelion. Then have her illustrate her findings in the second box on her recording sheet.
4. Have her examine what is left of her dandelion and draw a picture of it in the third box on her recording sheet.
5. Help her estimate how many seeds are left on her dandelion. Have her circle the appropriate number set on her recording sheet.
6. Preserve each child's creation by placing the square of Con-Tact paper atop the canvas to seal in the scattered seeds. Arrange all the squares in a quilt formation on a bulletin board display titled "Our Dandy Seed Quilt."

This is why: Each dandelion seed has its own tiny parachute of downy hairs that helps it fly through the air. When a dandelion flower head goes to seed, the stem of the flower stands up tall and straight to increase the chances of each seed being caught by the wind. The wind can carry some dandelion seeds for miles.

Suggested book: *The Dandelion Seed* by Joseph Anthony

Dandy Seeds

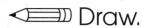 Draw.

I blew on my dandelion *gently:*

I blew on my dandelion *hard:*

After I blew on my dandelion it looked like this:

Circle.

My dandelion has this many seeds left:

    0   1–5   6–10   more than 10

Just Bloomin'

Youngsters' science skills will blossom as they participate in this plant part study!

Purpose: To help students understand the major parts of a plant

Background: The most common type of plant is a *flowering plant.* Flowering plants have four main parts: roots, stems, leaves, and flowers. The roots hold the plant in the soil and supply the plant with water and minerals from the soil. The stem usually supports the leaves and flower. The leaves take in sunlight and use it to combine water, carbon dioxide, and minerals to make food for the plant. The flower contains the parts needed to create more plants.

Getting started: Gather the materials listed below and take youngsters outdoors. Remove the plant from the pot and identify the parts of the plant as students observe. Discuss the function of each plant part (see the background information). Then help small groups of youngsters follow the steps below to complete the activity.

Materials:
copy of page 34 attached to a piece of cardboard for each child
flowering plant in a pot
crayons

Steps:
1. Help each small group of children find a flowering plant on the school grounds. (If desired, purchase a tray of seedlings from a garden center and give each group one seedling section.)
2. Have each child illustrate the plant on his recording sheet. Then read the labels on the page to students. Guide each child to draw a line from each label to the appropriate plant part.
3. Have each child observe the roots on the potted plant. Then guide each child in drawing the roots in the space provided on the sheet.
4. Invite each group to share its illustrations and then compare the similarities and differences in the plants observed.

This is why: Different flowering plants still have the same basic parts—roots, stems, leaves, and flowers.

Suggested book: *From Seed to Plant* by Gail Gibbons

The Parts of a Flowering Plant

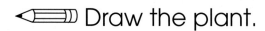 Draw the plant.

leaves	

stem	||

flowers	

 Draw the roots.

roots	

"Tree-mendous" Bark!

Science skills will be on the mark when youngsters discover the importance of bark!

Purpose: To help students understand how bark protects trees

Background: Bark is the outer covering of most trees, which shields the stem, roots, and branches from injury, insects, disease, and loss of water. New layers of bark grow every year, causing the outermost bark of most trees to become thick, rough, and scaly.

Getting started: Take youngsters on a walk around the school grounds and examine the bark on the trees. Ask students to identify the part of their bodies that serves as a protective covering *(skin).* Explain to youngsters that the bark of a tree is a protective covering for the inside of a tree just as our skin is a protective covering for the insides of our bodies. Invite students to gently feel the bark of a tree and compare it to their own skin. Then help pairs of students follow the steps below to complete the activity.

Materials for each child:
copy of page 36
brown crayon with wrapper removed

Steps:
1. Have one child in each pair hold a recording sheet against the bark of a tree while the other child uses the side of a crayon to make a rubbing.
2. Ask partners to switch roles and then make a rubbing of a different tree on the other recording sheet.
3. Gather youngsters together and examine the rubbings. Guide students to compare differences in the rubbings; then explain the differences (see below).
4. Help each child evaluate the age of his tree according to the condition of its bark; then have him circle his conclusion on his recording sheet.

This is why: Young trees have thin, smooth bark that creates a less textured rubbing. Most older trees have thick, rough, scaly bark that creates a rubbing with more texture.

Suggested book: *A Tree Is a Plant* by Clyde Robert Bulla

"Tree-mendous" Bark!

Listen for directions.

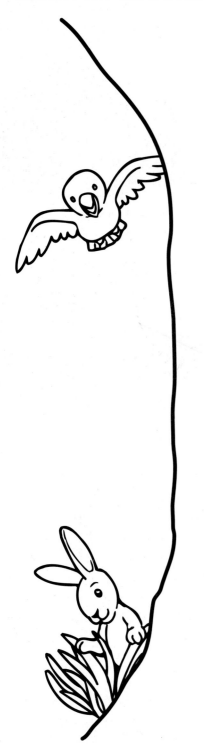

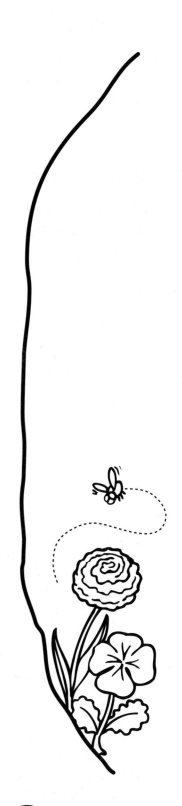

This tree is  young.

This tree is old.

Incredible Insects

Youngsters will go buggy over this insect investigation!

Purpose: To help students understand the characteristics of insects

Background: An insect is a small animal with six legs, a body with three main parts (head, thorax, and abdomen), and a tough outer covering (exoskeleton). Many insects have wings and a pair of antennae. Scientists who study insects (entomologists) have identified over 1 million different species of insects. Insects live almost everywhere on Earth, from the hottest areas to the coldest.

Getting started: Take your little entomologists outdoors for an insect hunt and ask them to observe insects (remind students not to touch any insect). Then help them follow the steps below to complete the activity.

Materials:
copy of page 38 attached to a piece of cardboard for each child
crayons

Steps:
1. Guide each child to notice whether each insect he observes has wings or not. Help him make a tally mark in the corresponding box on the sheet to record each winged and wingless insect observed.
2. Ask each child to draw in the jar at least five different insects he observes.
3. Discuss with students the similarities and differences of the various insects observed. Guide students to compare the size, color, body parts, and behavior of several insects.

This is why: More than any other type of animal, insects have a great variety in their size, color, and form. There are insects in every color of the rainbow. There are very tiny insects (fairy flies measure around $\frac{1}{100}$ of an inch in length) and giant insects (the wingspans of Atlas moths measure about ten inches). Many insects have wings, which help them search for food, escape from enemies, and find mates.

Suggested book: *Bugs Are Insects* by Anne Rockwell

Name _____

Just Buggy!

✏️ Draw.   I saw these insects:

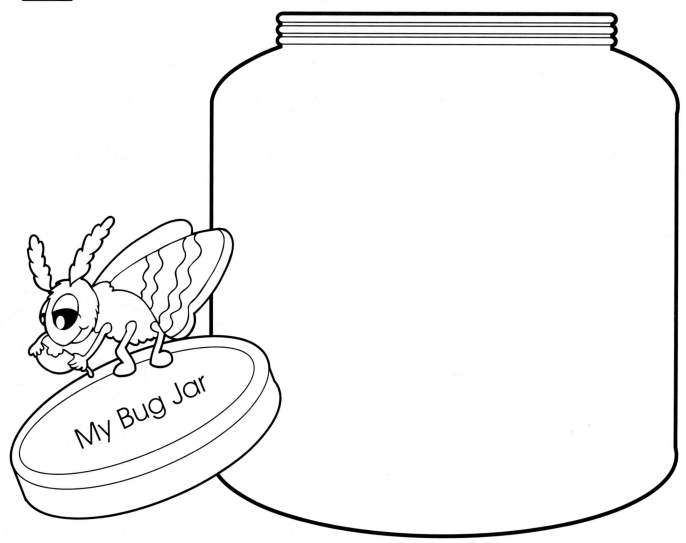

My Bug Jar

Tally.

Insects With Wings	Insects Without Wings

Wiggly Worms

Experiment

Youngsters will wiggle with excitement as they discover the importance of earthworms!

Purpose: To help students understand that earthworms help soil and need to live in damp soil

Background: Earthworms can be found below the surface of warm, moist soil throughout the world. Earthworms help soil by loosening and mixing it as they move, supplying air to it, and fertilizing it.

Getting started: Gather worms or purchase them from a fishing store. Place the worms on a damp paper towel and invite youngsters to observe them. Discuss with youngsters where they might find earthworms. Then follow the steps below to set up and complete the experiment with youngsters.

Materials :
copy of page 40 for each child
supply of worms
2 clear plastic containers
2 sheets of clear plastic wrap with several airholes
2 rubber bands

moist potting soil
plastic spoon
several sticky dots
crayons

Steps:
1. Fill each container with moist soil. Label the containers "A" and "B."
2. Place an equal number of worms on top of the soil in each container. Cover each container with plastic wrap and secure it with a rubber band.
3. Set container A in a sunny spot outdoors. Set container B indoors, out of direct sunlight. Let the containers sit for several hours depending on the intensity of the sun in your area.
4. Remove the plastic wrap from container A. Have students observe as you use a spoon to carefully remove soil until a worm is visible. Help a student mark the location of the worm by placing a sticker on the outside of the container. Do the same to find and mark the location of each remaining worm.
5. Repeat Step 4 for container B.
6. Compare the depths at which worms were found in the containers. Guide youngsters to observe that the worms in container A dug deeper than the worms in container B.
7. Have each child illustrate the results on his recording sheet.

This is why: Worms breathe through their skin and need moist soil to live in to keep their skin moist. If a worm's skin dries out, it will not be able to breathe and will die. When the sun dried the top of the soil in container A, the worms dug deeper to reach moister soil. Since the soil in container B was not in sunlight, it did not dry out on top, so the worms stayed closer to the top of the container.

Suggested book: *Wonderful Worms* by Linda Glaser

Wiggly Worms

Draw to show where the worms were found.

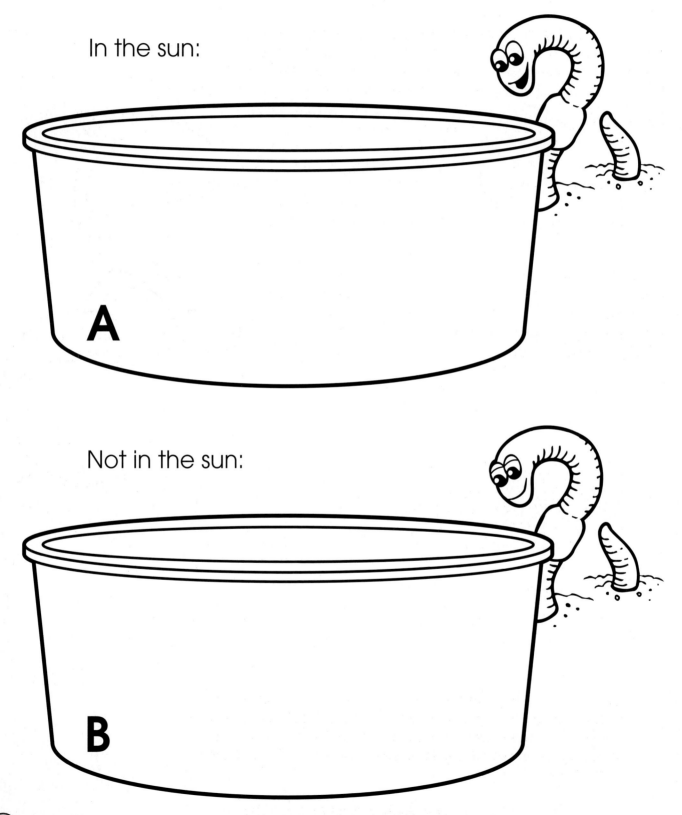

In the sun:

A

Not in the sun:

B

Drip, Drip, Drop

What's the chance for precipitation? One hundred percent with this soggy simulation activity.

Purpose: To help students understand how rain forms

Background: The sun's heat warms water from lakes, rivers, oceans, moist soil, and plants, causing it to evaporate, or turn into a gas. The evaporated water, called water vapor, rises into the air to form clouds. Warm air can hold more water vapor than cold air. When the air cools, the water vapor turns back into a liquid and raindrops begin to fall.

Getting started: On a cloudy day, take youngsters outside to observe clouds. Discuss the appearance of the clouds and how they form (refer to background information). Then help each small group follow the steps below to complete the activity.

Materials for each small group:
copy of page 42 for each child
crayons
clear plastic cup
moist potting soil (warmed in a microwave
   oven for one minute)

tablespoon
warm water
plastic wrap
rubber band
ice cube

Steps:
1. Give each group a cup of warmed soil.
2. Have one child in each group add two tablespoons of water to the cup.
3. Help each group tightly cover its cup with plastic wrap and then secure it with the rubber band as shown.
4. Guide students to notice the fog that forms in the cup. Then have each child draw the results on his recording sheet.
5. Have one child in each group gently place an ice cube on top of the plastic wrap. After about three minutes, water droplets will form inside the cup on the plastic wrap. As the ice cube melts, use a paper towel to soak up the excess water on top of the plastic wrap
6. Have each child draw the results on his recording sheet.

This is why: The heat from the soil in the cup causes water to evaporate and turn into water vapor. The ice cools the air inside the cup, and the water vapor begins to condense, or change into a liquid, forming droplets of water. When the droplets grow heavy, they fall as rain.

Suggested book: *This Is the Rain* by Lola M. Schaefer

Drip, Drip, Drop

 Draw your results.

Fish Wish

Demonstration

Introduce your little conservationists to the effects of water pollution with this fishy experiment.

Purpose: To help youngsters understand how water pollution affects nature

Background: Water is a natural resource that every living thing needs in order to survive. Water pollution is a serious environmental problem because it can affect the quality of life. Water pollution includes any substance that affects the natural condition of water, including industrial waste, sewage, oil, and agricultural chemicals and waste. Industrial waste includes chemicals and hot water. Sewage includes garbage, human waste, and soapy water.

Getting started: To prepare, cut a fish shape from each sponge and fill each container with water. Discuss with youngsters the sources of water pollution and how pollution can affect people, plants, and animals. Take them outside to look for signs of pollution around the schoolyard, such as trash or oil on the street; then help them follow the steps below to complete the activity.

Materials:
copy of page 44 for each child
5 small sponges
5 clear plastic containers
shredded paper (to represent trash)
¼ cup cooking oil
a squirt of liquid soap
several drops of food coloring (to represent chemical pollutants)

Steps:
1. Ask a child to add shredded paper to one container. Then have another child put one fish in the container as young-sters observe. Discuss with students how trash may get into water and how it affects fish living in water. Encourage them to brainstorm ways to prevent this type of water pollution as you record their answers on a chart.
2. Repeat Step 1 with each remaining item (oil, soap, and food coloring) in a different container.
3. Have a child put a fish in the clean water container as youngsters observe. Discuss with youngsters how the water is different from the polluted water in the other containers.
4. Remove each fish and lay it next to its container. Allow youngsters to observe, touch, and compare each fish. Ask students to hypothesize which water would be healthier for the fish to live in. Then have each child draw to illustrate each sentence on her recording sheet.

This is why: Water pollution changes the *quality* (cleanliness, temperature, etc.), availability, and usefulness of water. Fish and other aquatic animals are sensitive to changes in their water environment.

Suggested book: *Precious Water: A Book of Thanks* by Brigitte Weninger

Name _____

Fish Wish

🖍 Draw.

A happy fish is in clean water.

🐟🐟🐟🐟🐟🐟🐟🐟🐟🐟🐟🐟🐟🐟

A sad fish is in polluted water.

Feathered Friends

Youngsters' observation skills will soar as they identify bird habitats in the schoolyard.

Purpose: To help students understand bird behavior through observation

Background: There are around 9,300 species of birds in the world. Birds share our environment more than any other animal, providing us with many opportunities for bird-watching. Birds usually follow a regular routine of feeding, preening, and bathing at the same time each day.

Getting started: In advance, determine an area outside where youngsters can clearly observe the sky, a tree, the ground, and a building. Discuss with youngsters different places in the schoolyard where birds can be seen. Tell students it is important to be quiet while bird-watching so the birds won't be scared away. Read the text on the journal page to youngsters. Take them outdoors with their journals at the same time for five consecutive days and help them follow the steps below to complete the activity.

Materials for each student:
5 copies of page 46 clipped onto a piece of cardboard
crayons

Steps:
1. Ask each child to record the day's weather by drawing in the box provided on the appropriate journal page.
2. Have each child look and listen quietly for birds for a few minutes.
3. Help him observe each area (sky, tree, ground, and building) and then record the number of birds observed by drawing them in the corresponding boxes.
4. When the group returns to the classroom, have each child count and record the total number of birds he has observed.
5. Repeat Steps 1–4 for four days, observing at the same time each day.
6. Review the results with the group to determine which area was the birds' favorite habitat around your school. Which area had the fewest birds? Did the weather affect the number of birds observed?

This is why: Bird-watching helps develop observation and identification skills. Recording where birds live in your neighborhood in a journal helps you become more observant of your surroundings.

Suggested book: *Amazing Birds* by Alexandra Parsons

Name _____

Feathered Friends Journal

 Draw.

Today's weather	Sky 
Tree	Ground
Building	How many birds did I see today?

Sun Blockers

Youngsters will shine with this picture-perfect way to explore the power of the sun!

Purpose: To help students understand how to protect themselves from overexposure to the sun

Background: The sun's ultraviolet rays affect many surfaces on Earth, including human skin. Too much exposure to UVB rays can cause a sunburn. To protect skin from harmful rays, limit exposure to the sun or cover the body with clothing or with sunscreen.

Getting started: Discuss with youngsters how the sun affects plants, animals, and people *(helps things grow, makes things warm, causes sunburn, etc.)*. On a bright sunny day, help youngsters follow the steps below to complete the activity.

Materials for each child:

copy of page 48　　　　　　　scissors
black construction paper　　　Sticky-Tac
red construction paper　　　　access to tape

Steps:

1. Help each child tape her copy of page 48 onto her black construction paper and then have her cut out the shapes.
2. Have her arrange the black shapes on her red construction paper to make a scene. Then help her use small bits of Sticky-Tac to hold the shapes in place.
3. Take youngsters outdoors and have each child set her paper in a sunny location. (To ensure that the paper does not blow away, place a pebble on each corner of it.)
4. Have students check the papers at the end of the day. Have each child carefully pull off one shape and observe the fading of the red paper. Then have her replace the shape and bring the paper indoors.
5. Repeat Steps 3 and 4 the next day.
6. Discuss how the energy from the sun changes the red construction paper. What happens to the areas exposed to sunlight? What happens to the areas covered by the black shapes?

Ashley

This is why: The areas covered by the black shapes stay red, while the exposed areas of the paper fade. The sun's rays do not penetrate the black paper to fade the red paper beneath it. Likewise, covering the skin with a layer of clothing or a layer of sunscreen will help to keep skin from being affected by overexposure to the sun.

Suggested book: *The Sun Is Always Shining Somewhere* by Allan Fowler

Shape Patterns

Summer: sun   ©The Education Center, Inc. • *Science in the Schoolyard* • TEC917

Water Wonders

Experiment

Watch students' science knowledge take shape with this fun water exploration activity.

Purpose: To help youngsters understand that water takes the shape of its container

Background: Water is the most common substance on the earth. Water covers over 70 percent of the surface of the earth, filling rivers, lakes, and oceans; it is also in the ground and in the air we breathe. Water is made up of many tiny, invisible parts called *molecules,* which are always moving. One drop of water has millions of molecules.

Getting started: On the sidewalk or another level area outside, fill several plastic tubs with water and tint each one with a different color of food coloring. (Give each small group a different tub.) Place the materials beside each tub. Then help each small group of youngsters follow the steps below to complete the activity.

Materials for each small group:
copy of page 50 clipped to a piece of cardboard for each child
crayons
several 8 oz. plastic measuring cups
several funnels
8 oz. plastic salad dressing bottle
8 oz. foam cup
8 oz. single-serving aluminum pie pan
(or substitute other 8 oz. containers: margarine, yogurt, or sour cream containers, plastic mustard bottles)

Steps:
1. Have each child choose a measuring cup and fill it with water.
2. Have each child choose a container and carefully pour the water from his measuring cup into it, using a funnel if necessary. Help him compare the shape of the container and the measuring cup. (Do not empty the water from the container.)
3. Have him refill his measuring cup. Then repeat Step 2 with two different containers.
4. Help him place the filled measuring cup and the three filled containers on a level area. Then compare each container. How are they the same? *(They each hold the same amount of water.)* How are they different? *(Each one has a different shape.)*
5. Help him record his findings by drawing the measuring cup and three containers, each on a separate section of his recording sheet.

This is why: Water is a liquid, which has no definite shape; therefore, it takes the shape of its container. The molecules in water move around freely and slide over each other. When you pour water into a container, it spreads out to cover the bottom and takes on that shape.

Suggested book: *Water* by Alice K. Flanagan

Name _____

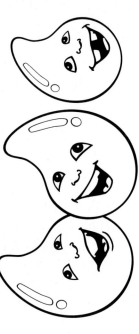

Water Wonders

Each container holds one cup of water.

✏️ Draw.

The containers are different shapes.
The amount of water is the same.

Cloud Patrol

Mobilize your students to be on the lookout for special types of clouds!

Purpose: To help students understand the different types of clouds

Background: Clouds are made up of clusters of water droplets or tiny ice crystals that float in the air. Three types of clouds are cumulus, which resemble fluffy cotton; stratus, which resemble flat gray sheets; and cirrus, which resemble feathers. Clouds are categorized by their shape, altitude, and potential to produce rain or snow.

Getting started: Show students pictures of the different types of clouds (see suggested book below). Discuss the different shape and name of each cloud with youngsters. Show children some puffy cotton balls to illustrate cumulus clouds. Do the same with a feather to illustrate cirrus clouds and a gray sheet of paper to illustrate stratus clouds. Then take youngsters outside to observe clouds and then record their findings.

Materials:
copy of page 52 clipped to a piece of cardboard for each student
cotton balls
feather
sheet of gray paper
crayons

Steps:
1. Ask youngsters to observe the sky and look for clouds. Help them identify the type of cloud they observe. Have each child draw the cloud on his recording sheet. Help him circle the corresponding cloud icon to show the type of cloud. Then have him draw to record the weather for that day.
2. Help students repeat Step 1 for four more days.
3. Review the results with youngsters. Ask students to look at their recording sheets to determine whether a certain type of weather appeared each time a certain type of cloud appeared. For example, did they see stratus clouds on a rainy day, or was there a thunderstorm when cumulus clouds were piled up high in the sky?

This is why: Cirrus clouds are made up of ice crystals that hang high in the sky. Cumulus clouds may rise high in the sky and bring thunderstorms. Stratus clouds are like a thick gray blanket that covers the sky, and they usually bring rain or snow.

Suggested book: *The Cloud Book* by Tomie dePaola

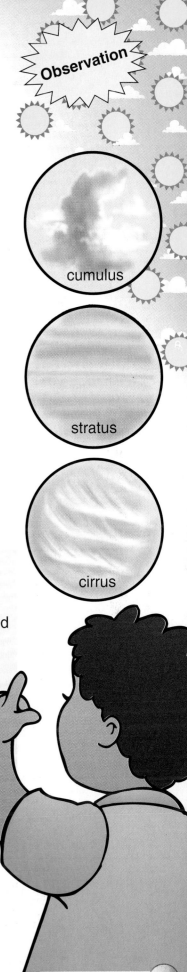

cumulus

stratus

cirrus

Name _____

Cloud Patrol

🖍 Draw the cloud you see.

✏️ Circle the cloud it looks like.

🖍 Draw today's weather.

Today the weather is...

Day 1	
Day 2	
Day 3	
Day 4	
Day 5	

Bubbles All Round

Gather round for a shapely investigation of soapy spheres!

Purpose: To help students understand that bubbles floating in the air are always round

Background: A soap bubble forms when air is pushed against a thin layer of soap film. The film traps the air inside it, forming a tiny chamber of air: a bubble.

Getting started: To prepare for this investigation, gather six pipe cleaners. Make bubble wands by bending each pipe cleaner into one of the shapes shown on page 54. Then take youngsters outdoors and help them follow the steps below to complete the activity.

Materials:
copy of page 54 clipped to a piece of cardboard for each child
pipe cleaner bubble wands in various shapes
bubble solution in a large, shallow container
crayons

Steps:
1. Show youngsters the bubble solution and the wands. Give each child a copy of the recording sheet and a crayon.
2. Ask each child to predict what shape bubble will be blown from the circle bubble wand. Have her illustrate her answer on her recording sheet in the "I Predict" column next to the picture of the circle wand.
3. Invite one child to blow a bubble using the circle wand. Ask youngsters to observe the shape of the bubble. Then have each child record the shape of the bubble in the corresponding "I See" column on her sheet.
4. Repeat Steps 2 and 3 with each remaining bubble wand shape. Encourage students to think about what they have observed before they make each prediction.
5. Discuss youngsters' predictions and the actual results.

This is why: Bubbles floating in the air are always round. The air inside the bubble pushes out evenly in all directions against the soap skin of the bubble. At the same time, the soap skin pushes back against the air, making the bubble round.

Suggested book: *Pop! A Book About Bubbles* by Kimberly Brubaker Bradley

Bubble Shapes

✏️ Draw.

Wand	I Predict	I See
circle		
square		
triangle		
star		
rectangle		
heart		

Bubble-O!

Slip-Sliding Away

Youngsters will get carried away with this erosion activity.

Purpose: To help students understand the process of erosion

Background: Erosion is a natural process in which rock and soil are broken into smaller pieces and gradually moved to a different location. One of the major causes of erosion is the movement of water. For example, raindrops splashing against a hill will move soil particles downhill. Although erosion can occur gradually over millions of years, erosion can also occur rapidly, such as when water flows down sloping land not covered by grass or plants.

Getting started: Invite youngsters outside to search for an area in which erosion is evident. Have students examine the eroded area and discuss their observations. Lead students to notice that soil is composed of small particles that can be broken down by rubbing them between their hands. Then help youngsters follow the steps below to complete the activity.

Materials:

copy of page 56 for each child
2 large tubs
soil
water
large cup

watering can
brown watercolor paint
paintbrushes
crayons

Steps:

1. Firmly pack one side of each tub with soil to form a sloping hill.
2. Have each child illustrate the hill in the first box on her recording sheet.
3. Ask students to predict what will happen when rain (water from the watering can) is sprinkled over one of the hills.
4. Help a student sprinkle water over one hill as the class observes.
5. Have each child paint in the corresponding box on her sheet to illustrate the results.
6. Ask students to predict how a flow of water will affect the hill.
7. Help a student pour a large cup of water over the hill in the other tub.
8. Have each child paint in the corresponding box on her sheet to illustrate the results.

This is why: More soil was moved by the water that was poured from the cup onto the hill than was moved by the sprinkling water. Compare this to the erosion caused by rain. Normal rainfall causes small amounts of soil to move downhill, while strong rainstorms move larger amounts of soil downhill, causing greater erosion.

Suggested book: *Erosion* by Rebecca Olien

Name _____

Slip-Sliding Away

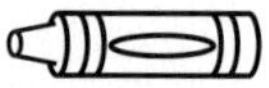

Hill

Shower

Flow

Summer: soil

Hard As Rock

Your amateur rock collectors will enjoy this rocky investigation!

Purpose: To help students understand that rocks can be classified by their hardness

Background: Hardness is one way to classify minerals in rocks. Hardness can be estimated by scratching a mark on a rock with an object such as a penny or a fingernail. Scientists measure hardness of a rock by comparing it with *Mohs' scale,* a table of ten well-known minerals arranged in order from one (talc) to ten (diamond).

Getting started: In advance, gather several different types of rocks for the class to observe and compare. You may want to obtain a rock identification book for reference, such as *Rocks and Minerals* by Steve Parker. Take youngsters outside to collect a variety of rocks and then help a small group at a time follow the steps below to complete the activity.

Materials for each group:
copy of page 58 for each child
rock and mineral collection (5 rocks per child)
damp paper towels
pennies (1 per child)
index cards (5 per child)
magnifying glass
crayons

Steps:
1. Have each child clean her rock collection with a damp paper towel.
2. Help each child number her cards from 1 to 5 and then place one rock on each card. Encourage her to use a magnifying glass to observe the details of each rock.
3. Ask each child to draw each rock in the space provided next to the corresponding number on her sheet.
4. Help each child test one rock by trying to scratch it with a penny.
5. Help each child test the same rock by trying to scratch it with her fingernail. Place the rock back onto its numbered card.
6. Guide each child to record the results on her sheet.
7. Repeat Steps 4–6 with each remaining rock.
8. Help each child refer to her recording sheet to sort her rock collection by those that can be scratched by a penny or a fingernail and those that cannot be scratched by either one.

This is why: If a rock cannot be scratched by a fingernail, then it is harder than a fingernail. If a rock cannot be scratched by a penny, then it is harder than a penny. Some examples of soft minerals and rocks that are easily scratched are graphite (found in most pencils), gypsum, halite, soapstone, and sandstone.

Suggested book: *Let's Go Rock Collecting* by Roma Gans

Name _____

Hard As Rock

✏️ Draw your (rock.)   Did it get scratched?

🖍️ Color to show your answer.

Rock 1	penny 😊 ☹️ fingernail 😊 ☹️
Rock 2	penny 😊 ☹️ fingernail 😊 ☹️
Rock 3	penny 😊 ☹️ fingernail 😊 ☹️
Rock 4	penny 😊 ☹️ fingernail 😊 ☹️
Rock 5	penny 😊 ☹️ fingernail 😊 ☹️

Let It Slide

Slide into the study of motion with this moving experiment!

Purpose: To help youngsters understand that the distance a moving object travels is affected by the texture of the surface it is on

Background: Motion occurs when an object changes its location. *Friction* (the force that opposes the motion of an object) from different surface textures affects the speed of a moving object. Objects travel more easily on smooth surfaces than on rough surfaces.

Getting started: In advance, prepare a sliding ramp by drawing a green, a yellow, and a red circle on a long piece of smooth cardboard; then prop it up on several books as shown. Take youngsters outside to slide down the playground sliding board. Ask them to hypothesize why they traveled fast or slow down the playground slide. Then help each child in a small group follow the steps below to complete the activity.

Materials:
copy of page 60 for each child
3 different-textured testing materials
   sized to cover the ramp (terry cloth
   beach towel, paper towels, bubble
   wrap, waxed paper, sandpaper, carpet,
   fabric, aluminum foil, etc.)

1" square of each testing material
   for each child
crayons
toy vehicle for each child
glue

Steps:
1. Test the slant of the sliding ramp by having each child place his vehicle at the top (next to the green circle) and release it. Add more books, if needed, to change the slant of the board.
2. Have each child prepare his recording sheet by coloring the circles on each pictured ramp. Then have him glue one sample of each testing material in the box provided.
3. Place one testing material on the ramp.
4. Have one child at a time place his vehicle on the ramp and release it. Encourage him to give oral observations of the experience, such as "My car stopped between the yellow and red circles." Then have him record the position where his vehicle stopped by drawing a picture of it in the appropriate place on his sheet.
5. Repeat Steps 3 and 4 for the other two testing materials.
6. Discuss youngsters' results. Which material made the vehicles go fast, and which material made them slow down?

This is why: The amount of friction from the surface depends on the materials used on the ramp. The toy vehicle will travel farther on a smooth surface because there is less resistance than on rough surfaces.

Suggested book: *Push and Pull* by Patricia J. Murphy

Name _____

Let It Slide

©The Education Center, Inc. • *Science in the Schoolyard* • TEC917

Float My Boat

This sink or float experiment will have students saying, "Oh, buoy!"

Purpose: To help students understand the concepts of sink and float

Background: Objects float or sink in water depending on their density. *Density* is the weight of an object according to its size. For example, a golf ball is smaller than a beach ball, but a golf ball is more dense. Objects that are less dense than water will float. Objects that are denser than water sink because they weigh more than the amount of water they *displace.*

Getting started: After a summer shower, take youngsters outside to find a puddle. Ask them to describe what might happen if a beach ball were dropped in the puddle. Then have them describe what might happen if a penny were dropped in the puddle. Invite students to hypothesize why objects sink or float. Then help a small group of students follow the steps below to complete the activity.

Materials for each small group:
copy of page 62 for each child
pencil for each child
small ball of modeling clay for each child
supply of counters
large plastic container filled with water

Steps:

1. Have the group sit around the plastic container.
2. Ask each child to predict if her ball of clay will sink or float and then record her prediction on her recording sheet.
3. Invite each child to drop her clay into the water and then record the result on her sheet.
4. Have each child mold her ball of clay into a boat shape, predict if it will sink or float, and then record her prediction.
5. Invite her to set her boat in the water and then record the result.
6. Direct each child to predict how many counters it will take to sink her boat; then have her record her prediction on her sheet.
7. Have each child place counters in her boat until it sinks and then record the results on her sheet.

This is why: The ball of clay is *dense,* or heavy for its size, so it sinks in the water. When the clay is stretched into a boat shape it displaces more water, so it floats. Adding counters to the boat increases its density and causes it to sink.

Suggested book: *Who Sank the Boat?* by Pamela Allen

Float or Sink?

🖍 Color.

	Predict		Result	
	sink	float	sink	float
🍪				
🥣				

How many will sink the 🥣 ?

predict

result

Hearts Are Pumping

How will your students rate this heart exploration? Two "thumps" up!

Purpose: To help students understand the function of the heart

Background: Exercise helps make the body strong and healthy. The heart is a muscle that pumps blood throughout the body, carrying oxygen and food to all parts of the body. A person's heart rate, or *pulse,* automatically increases or decreases according to the body's needs. For example, the heart pumps slowly when we are sleeping, but it pumps fast while we are exercising.

Getting started: In advance, draw an activity of your choice in the blank box on a copy of page 64 and then make a class supply of the recording sheet. Help each child find his pulse on his neck as shown. Explain that a person's pulse indicates how fast or slow his heart is pumping. Then take youngsters outside to get a little exercise as they follow the steps below to complete the activity.

Materials:
copy of page 64 attached to a piece of cardboard for each child
crayons
jump rope to share

Steps:
1. Find a place for students to sit in a circle on the playground.
2. Discuss how exercise affects the heart rate. Then demonstrate heart rate by clapping slowly to illustrate a slow pulse and clapping quickly to illustrate a fast pulse (normal rate for a child is about 90 beats per minute).
3. Have each child check his pulse and then record whether his pulse is slow or fast by coloring the appropriate icon on his recording sheet.
4. Have students walk around an area of the playground for a short period of time. Then have each child check his pulse and then record whether his pulse is slow or fast by coloring the appropriate icon on his sheet.
5. Have students repeat Step 4 for each remaining activity.
6. Ask students to sit quietly for a few moments to let their heart rates slow down. Then have them check their pulses again.
7. Discuss how the different activities affected the students' heart rates.

This is why: During vigorous activities, such as running, the body needs more oxygen, so the heart pumps faster to provide more oxygen-rich blood to the body. When the body slows down and rests, the heart pumps more slowly because less oxygen is needed throughout the body.

Suggested book: *Exercise* by Sharon Gordon

Fast or Slow?

 Color to show your results.

©The Education Center, Inc. • *Science in the Schoolyard* • TEC917